MW01232856

COMMON PLACES

Poems of Everyday Encounters

AVAR HURD JAMES

WESTBOW
P R E S S®
A DIVISION OF THOMAS NELSON
& ZONDERVAN

WestBow Press books may be ordered through booksellers or by contacting:

WestBow Press
A Division of Thomas Nelson & Zondervan
1663 Liberty Drive
Bloomington, IN 47403
www.westbowpress.com
844-714-3454

ISBN: 978-1-6642-8423-4 (sc)
ISBN: 978-1-6642-8424-1 (hc)
ISBN: 978-1-6642-8422-7 (e)

Library of Congress Control Number: 2022921384

Print information available on the last page.

WestBow Press rev. date: 12/02/2022

In memory of
my parents, Leon and Doris Hurd, Sr.
. and my grandmother, Avar Pipkin
They were instrumental role models who
taught me much about life.
Their impact has left indelible marks on my heart and mind.
Their influence is a priceless and precious treasure.

INTRODUCTION

Life is a journey filled with ups and downs. Obligations and responsibilities come with it. We, however, often get stuck in ruts and routines. We must interrupt the existing regimen to appreciate the simple things – the things that do not cost anything except time. What a difference this can make at the end of the day. Hobbies, pastimes, family and friends, bring much needed pleasures which result in lasting memories.

"Take time to smell the roses" is a familiar expression. Part of the beauty of the rose is its fragrance. To smell it adds to its uniqueness and enhances appreciation of its beauty. We must slow down and enjoy the simple pleasures.

Common places: places where we all have been, things we all have seen and done, are familiarities and experiences that make life what it is. Common places: the simple acts of enjoying the wonders of our world, are essential for the journey.

CONTENTS

Taken For Granted

A Mixed Bag

My Journey

FROM THE BEGINNING

From the beginning,
this created earth was filled with
dynamic and different forms seen in mountains
and hills, oceans and rivers, plains and grasslands,
beauty in nature with varied colors of trees,
flowers, and shrubs,
the intricate workings of the human body,
birds, fish, and animals,
the seasons with their visible variations,
the clouds, sun, moon, and stars.
The beauty and wonder of this diverse and
magnificent world give voice to the poems in this
section of the book.

BABIES

Babies are a gift from God
Bless their precious little hearts

No matter if it's a girl or boy
Their beginnings bring such joy

Without a word or mention
Their presence demands full attention

Babies are tender and soft to touch
You want to caress them so much

The itty- bitty fingers and toes
The cute little button nose

The adorable little baby face
Their existence warms the place

They're so cuddly and small
A precious blessing, after all

Remember the burps, smiles and tears
For they are infants for too few years

Make memories that will last
Because they grow up much too fast

BIRDS

I like to hear the chirping
From the backyard tree
It is such a refreshing sound
That often awakens me

I am not a bird watcher
Not by any means
But I do await the cuties
I want them to be seen

I gaze out the kitchen window
And see one that has perched
They never stay put for long
Darting off in their search

Often not there long enough
To be able to identify
For it appears in just a blink
They are soaring toward the sky

I saw a cardinal this morning
Birds delight me so
They add much to nature
Everywhere they go

CHICKEN

I like chicken, don't you
I don't know which I like best
I 've put many dishes to the test

Roasted, baked, or fried
Gumbo, soups, and pot pies
Dumplings and stews
Stuffed and bar-be-qued
Sandwiches, wraps, and salads too
And don't forget the wings and cordon bleu

I could eat chicken every day
If prepared a different way
I fix it much, it's so versatile
The hubby grows weary, though, after a while

CLAY

Clay from the earth, buff, red, mostly gray
Mixed with just water becomes a beautiful display

Clay mixed and shaped by the potter's hand
Becomes his own creation, be it petite or grand

Crafted, it makes porcelain, earthen or stoneware
Bricks, flowerpots, bowls, vases and dinnerware

The shapeless blob of clay once worked and fired
So colorful and decorated as the potter is inspired

DIAMONDS

Diamonds are made of carbon
Fashioned into gems
It takes skill and ingenuity
To process all of them

Diamonds are formed
From pressure underground
Slowly pushed from the depths
Is where diamonds are found

Diamonds are blasted, dug and crushed
Still, though, they are diamonds in the rough
Until washed, sorted, cut
And polished to a buff

The cut and the polish
Let its beauty shine through
With no imperfections
Bringing its purity into view

The most precious and costliest
Of all the jeweled things
Associated with life's happiest moments
For a bride's wedding ring

It has been said that
Diamonds are a girl's best friend
This hardest natural substance
Will endure to the end

FLOWERS

Nature would be so very bland
Without flowers to adorn the land

Flowers are beautiful to view
And quite useful, too

Flowers most often decorate
Places one wishes to celebrate

Roses, violets, irises and mums
Daffodils, tulips and daises are some

Colored red, yellow, pink, violet and white
Flowers bring much delight

They brighten every occasion
A perfumed and fragrant inspiration

In centerpieces, potted or in a vase
In yards and gardens to suit ones taste

Picked by hand or bought in stores
Flowers speak love and much more

FRUITS AND VEGGIES

Supplying produce is a tedious process
Methodically and specifically in each case
Cultivating, planting, weeding, watering
And fertilizing have to take place

Farming is hard and strenuous work
Requiring effort, patience, and time
Yet what results from diligence
Is an assortment that is by design

A plethora of color and shapes, too
Displayed in red, yellow, purple, orange, and green
In the most impressive section of the marketplace
A vibrant year-round harvest can be seen

An array of deliciousness for customers to view
Crops grown from roots, leaves, stems, and seeds
To produce nutritious quality and freshness
Choose those that suit your needs

A variety of fruits and veggies
Is recommended for us each day
To thrive, stay healthy and grow
Consuming them daily is the best way

GO TO THE ANT

Go to the ant, consider its ways and be wise
For there is much to learn as God's word does advise

Ants are such amazing and complex little creatures
Their lives are so structured, one of its noted features

Individually, they are organized and smart
Collectively, as a unit, each doing his part

Ants modify their habitats and use available resources
They go about undisturbed following the lead of older forces

Their diligent work ethics are an inspiration
No wonder they're referenced for arduous work and cooperation

This tiny little insect surely does fascinate
How they live and work, we would do well to imitate

GRANDKIDS

Grandkids are special
They really are
They are your children's kids
That is who they are

Once you have them
You will understand
How unique they are
And why they are called "grand"

We repeat their words
We like what they do
We share their pictures
And their fun times, too

When with you at home
A mess they can make
But time spent with them
You would not forsake

God made grandkids
For grandparents to enjoy
They brighten our days
And bring so much joy

Kiss them and hug them
And spoil if you must
They are God's gift
And to us He entrusts

HANDS

The most useful tool of man are his hands
With them, there is much we do
Allow me then, to name a, few

You can lend a hand or hand someone something
You can hold a hand or with someone you can cling

You can shake a hand, open a door or make a bed
Point a finger, drive a car, brush your teeth,
or comb the hair on your head

You can use your hands to lace a shoe or bake a cake
Blow kisses, wave good-bye, set things down or pick up to take

You can raise your hand, clap or keep them to yourself
Use a vacuum, a broom, or to clean a dusty shelf

With hands you polish nails or handwrite a note
You can text, email, hold the phone, or cast a vote

Adorn with rings, hold onto a rail, put in pocket or purse
Stick them in the cookie jar or write your own verse

Wring your hands, put on gloves, use tools to build or mold
Put clothes in the dryer and take them out to fold

Open the fridge, turn on the lights and
stop the alarm clock at dawn
Make sandcastles, build snowmen, and cover when you yawn

Our hands should be appreciated
We use them so much
Let us not take them for granted
And treat them as such

LAUGHTER

Laughter is the best medicine
We have been told
It has health benefits
For the body and soul

Laughter stimulates lungs and heart
It stretches muscles in the face
Soothing tension and reducing stress
A hearty laugh enlivens, in any case

Laughter dulls the pain and helps one to sleep
It boosts your mood and lightens your load
Creating happiness and joy
Increasing memory and learning modes

Chuckle, giggle, and belly laugh
Make for a pleasant sound
It is infectious and contagious
When these expressions abound

Laughter makes the world go round
Laugh loud, laugh long, take a laughing break
A valuable asset to have
For well-being and for goodness sakes

MOUNTAINS

A mountain is more than
A large mass of land
That rises high above the land around it

Where you are
Determines your perspective

Perhaps you are down in the valley
And would prefer to be on the mountain
Whether you have made
A mountain out of a molehill
Or if you have a mountain to climb
Or if you have a mountain of issues
Or your mountain seems too high
Or the mountain does not come to you

If

You have enough faith
You can speak to the mountain
And the mountain will move
And you will experience a mountain high
And relish in your mountain-top experience

SALT

Salt had many uses back in the ancient days
In oil lamps, as an antiseptic, and part of soldiers' pay
As a rub for newborns to ensure good health
As the chief economic product, a source of wealth

Salt has gotten a bad rap
Because too much is used
In chips, packaged foods, and snacks
And especially in canned goods

Too much salt
Has some unhealthy effects
It elevates blood pressure
Increases strokes and heart attacks

However, salt is a nutrient
Essential for our health
An important part of blood
Vital to the stomach
Helps water retention
Stimulates muscle contraction
Keeps the body balances
And aids in digestion

Only in moderation
Should salt be used
It is easier to add salt
Than it is to remove

Salt has its value
That cannot be overlooked
Too much salt is not good
Consume only what you should

SEASONS

New frocks, bonnets, and bright-colored eggs
Flowers in bloom and time to spring ahead
Billowing trees, green grass, and bumble bees
Allergies and pollen that make you sneeze
It's starting to get warm!

Parks and vacation, time out-of-school
Beach towels, sun lotion, and swimming pools
Watermelon, bar-be-que, and lemonade
Baseball, lawn chairs, and looking for shade
It's starting to get hot!

Time to give thanks, festivals, and pumpkin pies
Colored leaves, corn mazes and hayrides
Time to fall back, apple cider and hot tea
It's football time in Tennessee
It's starting to get cool!

Birds fly south, barren trees and fluffy snow
Blankets, throws, covered furniture on the patio
Gift giving, fireplaces and basketball
Hats, coats, earmuffs, and shawls
It's starting to get cold!

Thank God for whatever his reason
That He brings us the seasons
And all the changes they bring
In winter, fall, summer, and spring

SLEEP

Sleep, sleep
Beautiful sleep

Nothing can replace
A good night's sleep

God purposed it that way
He knew what the body would need

To energize and recharge
To get a fresh start
To begin a new day
To work in a rested way

Sleep, sleep
Beautiful sleep

THE COLOR OF GREEN

Green may not be primary on the color wheel
Yet it is dominant and very present, still

Imagine a world with green nowhere
Surely, gloom and dreariness would be there

Think of green grass, plants, shrubs, and trees
How barren and drab it would be without these

Greens, salads, spinach, broccoli, and kale
All green veggies provide nourishment, without fail

Green signals "go" in traffic signs
Giving the go-ahead as created by design

Green is the color of dollar bills
Indicative of stability and growth that money gives

Green symbolizes life, freshness, and peace
Evoking harmony and good health which are released

Of all the colors that grace our Earth
Green, more than any other, has its worth

In nature, environment, food, and cash
Green adorns and lets its beauty unlash

THE COLOR OF RED

Red is primary on the color wheel
From it other colors are made
Red summons your attention
Regardless of the shade

Think of many things
That are the color red
Compared with other colors
Red is far ahead

The color red is popular
It's intense, powerful, and bold
Symbols, signals, and indicators
This color does control

Red is life and vitality
Symbolizing love and even hate
Red is warmth and it is heat
Energy it does radiate

To be without red might seem strange
Things just would not be the same
Because of the dominance
This color red claims

THE DAISY

The daisy is the second largest of flowering plants
This birth flower of April that symbolizes innocence

The most common daisy petals are pure white
With a bright yellow center, a crisp fresh delight

The "days eyes" as they appear closes at night
But the petals open again in the morning light

Daises make childhood jewelry tied together in a chain
And when used as vase fillers their beauty reigns

The way to determine "he loves me, he loves me not"
One plucks the daisy's petal to determine her lot

Daisies are perennials and convey modesty and cheer
Yet farmers consider them weeds and want them nowhere near

Because they are perennials, they do not die
The simple little daisy – each day it greets the sky

THE GOOD LIFE

EaT Right
Help OtHers
Exercise

Give Generously
HOnor God
COmplain Little
Apply the GolDen Rule

Show Love
Enjoy LivIng
Laugh OFten
Do Your BEst

THE HUMAN HEART

The human heart is something
Only God could create
All that it does for the body
The way it operates

Intricately and marvelously made
To pump blood throughout
To carry oxygen and nutrients
To tissues spread about

One of the most important organs
Of the entire body
Beating seventy-two times a minute
Helps our bodies function properly

The auricles and the ventricles
The chambers of the heart
The capillaries, aorta, and valves
All working to do their part

It's absolutely amazing how the heart works
Repeatedly without skipping a beat
Perfectly working and perfectly designed
It's an incredible God-created feat

THE MUSTARD SEED

The mustard seed is smallest
Of all of nature's seeds
Yet it far outgrows others
With such enormous leaves

The little mustard seed
Fulfills a basic need
The nutritional value is high
For oils and proteins they supply

Its size is the amount of faith one needs
And what can result if one believes
You can say to the mountain, "move"
Your entrusted faith will be proved

From this little bitty seed
Enormous outcomes may flow
God's power unleashes and lets go
Your mountain will not be where it was before

THE RAINBOW

If the rain is in front
And the sun is behind you
A brilliant order of color
A rainbow comes into view

The handcrafted arc of colors
That grace the sky
Lets you know for sure
That God is on high

Rainbows are a reminder
To all living things
That the world would never
Be destroyed by flood again

The order of colors
And what they symbolize
Creates a sense of wonder
So pleasant to visualize

Red, orange, yellow, green
Blue, indigo and violet
Appearing after the rain
But always before the sun

Created by God
A natural phenomenon

Rain
And, then
Instantaneously, a
Noticeable
Bowed
Order of color is
Witnessed

THE TONGUE

The tongue has many talents and though it's very small
We eat, swallow, taste and talk, this organ does it all

It is vital in eating food that we must chew
It jump-starts the digestive process, too

It helps when you need to lick a cone or lollipop
It aids in teaching loved ones, especially little tots

Taste buds help identify sour, salty and sweet
It determines texture, mushy, tough, or a crunchy treat

The tongue helps us all to sing and to speak
We must decide which words to say and which to keep

This powerful little muscle can build up or tear down
Always use it positively ---for peace and hope to abound

TREES

"Why do I like trees?" one might ask
Allow me to put your query to task

Trees are tall, green, majestic and grand
They grace and beautify the land

Trees cool the air as they provide shade
From the bountiful green leaves arrayed

For plants, birds and animals they provide
A comfortable place to reside

They hold houses where kids have fun
Warding off ultraviolet rays from the sun

Trees are used for timber production
Pulp for paper, for building and construction

Trees become furniture for the house
Wood is used, inside and all throughout

We get fuel needed for cooking and heating
Fruits, oils, seeds, and nuts for eating

So many products from wood you are aware
But there are several more to declare

I appreciate God's creation of trees
They beautify, they supply, they meet our needs

VEE FORMATION

The vee formation
Of Canadian geese
Evokes one's attention
And awe, to say the least

They speak of changing seasons
Flying south or north
And the value of teamwork
As they go soaring forth

What many may not know
If one must leave the vee
Be ill or wounded
Two go with him, making three

On the ground protected
Usually by the mate
Never left alone
At any rate

He is nurtured and cared for
To again fly
And if wounded beyond help
They stay until he dies

Then and only then
For efficiency and safety
They wait for another group
To rejoin the vee

WATER

To quench a thirst
It is water you want first

It's the best bottled drink
But can be used to fill the sink

To wash and rinse a dirty dish
Yet it fills a bowl for a little fish

With it we bathe and shower
And used also to water gardens and flowers

Farmers use it for irrigation
Water helps in food preparation

Freeze water to make ice
Boil and cook foods like rice

With it you brew coffee and tea
Without it, impossible to water ski

With water your teeth you brush
It is what makes the toilet flush

You fill and squirt water guns
Water parks need it in order to run

A must if you try to make jello
Or for the car to have a shiny glow

Water is required every single day
To wash dirt and germs away

Water is needed for us to survive
So, drink much, your body will thrive

TAKEN FOR GRANTED

There are numerous inventions, devices and products that have improved life tremendously for all. These advances have become second nature as we rely on them from day to day. Because they are so readily available and accessible, we tend to take these time and labor-saving things for granted, not giving much thought on how they impact our lives. Some of the poems give glimpses into life without these conveniences.

BATTERIES

Batteries are valuable
Worth their weight in gold
Just stop and think
About the power they hold

Batteries serve a purpose
Giving power to help things run
It's only when they stop
We realize their life is done

People depend on batteries
An awfully lot
You'd be surprised
At the number you got

They really are heavy duty
Be it A, AA, AAA, B, C, or D
We'd be in a bind without them
Wouldn't you agree

Cars, toys, tools, and remote controls
Just to a name a few
Watches, computers, alarms, toothbrushes
Heavy duty meaning does ring true

Christmas would not be the same
If no batteries could be found
No lithium or alkaline
Disappointment would certainly abound

So, the very next time
You replace a battery in a device
Give a nod for the power it has
The way it works is quite nice

BECAUSE OF THEM

It is important to remember and to celebrate
Black inventors who have much richness to embrace

They took the first steps to show the way
Their inventions have progressed us to this day

Not only were they the first in their fields
Some were slaves, uneducated, but so highly skilled

Limited by race but not by their wills
They have made an impact on society, even still

They had courage, fortitude, and strength of mind
For inventions that benefit all humankind

Folding chair, folding bed, curtain rod, and improved horseshoe
Stair climbing wheelchair, toilet, helicopter,
guitar, just to name a few

Almanac, blood bank, refrigerator, dustpan and mop
Paper bag production, camera, strongbox, - the list does not stop

Smoke detector, lasting machine, pencil sharpener and pen
Tube feeder, hydraulic press, corn planter – still no end

Roller coaster, traffic light, microphone,
clothes dryer and oil cup
Gas mask, lawn mower and inner tube – they did not give up

All the above- mentioned total a mere thirty-one
The list of inventions by Black Americans is nowhere done

There are many more conveniences and necessities, too
For Black inventors, gratitude and respect are due

Let us honor the achievements that we have here
Not just in February, but throughout the year

BOOKS

Books record information in permanent form
Kept in bookstores, libraries and homes
On shelves where they can be found
Or they can easily be carried around

Made from paper, print and publication
Books are a big part of education
Index, glossary, and table of contents
Help the insides make sense

Books are read all the time
Bringing information or pleasure to mind
They open doors to worlds unknown
Upon reading, knowledge is known

Even though technology has its place
Books have value and will not be replaced
The next time you open a book
Thank the editor for the opportunity he took

BRIDGES

Bridges are designed in construction
To overpass rivers, canyons, and other obstructions

Bridges speed traffic on their way
To avoid what would be a long delay

They are built to cross rivers and roads
And must be sturdy enough for heavy loads

Bridges do make life easier for us
Be it swing, suspension, wooden, or truss

To get from Point A to impassable Point B
The bridge makes it a possibility

So, the next time a bridge you must cross
Realize without it, you would be at a loss

COFFEE

Either you are a coffee lover, or you are not
If you are, you relish in that morning pot
Once perked, its aroma fills the place
I can hardly wait for that first taste

Some prefer regular or decaf
With sweetener or half and half
There is just something special in that mug
It makes the insides feel so snug

Coffee is a treat I want each day
It jumpstarts me on my way
A second cup or just a refill
Keeps the moment relaxed and still

That brown liquid is as good as gold
I see it and smell it in the cup I hold
So fulfilling, be it warm or hot
A cup of joe just hits the spot

The next time you sip to satisfy
Know that it is a pleasure that you cannot deny

ELECTRICITY

Electricity improves lives in many ways
Its labor-saving devices shorten our days
Wires and fields serve as its source
Connect by passing through wires in a course

Electricity provides us with heat
With stoves we cook food to eat
Irons, slow cookers, and electric frying pans
Readily heat with knobs on demand

Electricity provides refrigeration
Preserving food by preventing contamination
Freezers, fans, and air conditioners
Adjust from cool to cold positions

Electricity provides us with light
So even when it is dark, we have sight
Just let there be an outage of power
Life becomes frazzled in only one hour

Electric motors, vacuums and washing machines
Dryers, power tools and sewing machines
The listing could go on and on
With how our electric reliance has grown

From business, telephones, computers, and TVs
To manufacturing, industry and technology
There is one thing we can surely rule
Electricity is extremely "powerful"

HAVE A SEAT

You know what a seat is
And for what purpose it is used
But imagine life without it
You would be tired and confused

What would it be like
If you had nowhere to sit
If you stood all day long
Your body would have a fit

How would you watch TV at home
Would you stand and talk on the phone
At the table, how would you eat your meal
You'd never have to tell the kids to, "Sit still"

How would you listen to the preacher
Or take class notes from the teacher
What would you do at a football game
Or what would you do on an airplane

How would you drive a car
Don't think you'd get very far
How would moms manage with no highchair
How would the barber cut your hair

How would you sew at the machine
How would the dentist get your teeth clean
How could you be at a desk to compute
Or ride with others to commute

If there were no sofas, seats, or chairs
Life would be hard to bear
You would never say, "Have a seat"
Or "Come in and rest your feet"

If we all had to sit on the floor or ground
It would turn life upside down
So, the next time that you take a seat
Don't take it for granted, cause a seat is impossible to beat

MUSIC

The familiar phrase, "music to my ears"
Invokes pleasantries we like to hear

Music is universal, understood by everyone
Music has been instrumental since it has begun

Music is magical, it changes one's mood
Uplifting and inspiring, for the soul it is food

Music plays a big part in our daily lives
Listening to good music helps us grow and thrive

Music stirs emotions, calms, and invigorates
So many different feelings that music generates

Music helps us cope with all kinds of pain
It induces a meditative state for health, heart, and brain

So many genres, listen to what you choose
Be it classical, rock, jazz, rhythm, or blues

The beauty of music is what it communicates
Music to your ears will never be out-of-date

PAPER

Going paperless for printing is on the rise
With technological advances, it comes as no surprise
One can read a book, file a report, remit a bill,
Get a receipt, send a letter, or get a refill

Going paperless has some advantages
And benefits as well
But not everyone can or wants to go paperless
It's not always an easy sale

However, an interesting thought crossed my mind
What if no paper or paper products you could find
There would be no books, newspapers, or magazines
No need for printers, fax, or copy machines

There would be no cards, letters, or bills to send
And no use for pencils, inks, or pens
What would editors, authors, and publishers do
Librarians, teachers, and students, too

What if kids had no coloring books
And how would you show photos you took
What would you put in picture frames
Or play tic-tac-toe and board games

How would students take tests at school
For grade reporting, what would you use
How would you learn sheet music with notes
Or how would you remember a speech someone spoke

Missing items like paper towels and tissue
Could become a real issue
How would you shop at the grocery store
Without labels and product info

It would be hard to check out and escape
Without the use of check register tape
Receipts, checks, and prescriptions, also
Without paper, it is a no-go

And don't forget the dollar bill
It's made of paper too, be it fake or real
So, the next time you see paper around
Know that a million and one uses can be found

SUGAR

What if sugar were removed from all stores
And there would be no place to get more
Imagine some people would be upset
Cooks, bakers, and candy makers, I bet

What could be substituted in cookies, pies, ice cream and cake
Or any dishes like candied yams that you would make
How would you sweeten coffee, lemonade, or tea
Soda and fruit juices that have more sugar than needs to be

What would you dole out on Halloween for trick or treat
And Easter and Valentine's Day if there were no candy to eat
There is one I know who surely would not mind
For the dentist, fewer cavities he would find

We as a nation, though, consume way too much
Contributing to weight gain, health issues and such
Instead of removing all sugar, if we could use less
We would be better off and experience "sweet success"

THE AUTOMOBILE

When the rubber hits the road
I am ready to go
Imagine what life would be
Without the auto

Suppose all automobiles
Suddenly disappeared
It would erase this necessity
We have had for years

When I think back
To pre-vehicle days
To walking and horse-riding days
I am glad it is just a thought

Pieced together on an assembly line
An auto is manufactured in record time
The auto industry has changed our lives
Making for safer and smarter buys

Auto production provides millions of jobs
Evident by the number of cars on the road
Be it crossover, truck or van, pick-up, luxury or sedan

I take pleasure
In walking a few steps
Inserting the key
Starting my car
And going as I please

THE CAMERA

The camera was invented a long time ago
With each inventor improving what came before
Developed to have an image that would last
And to preserve the results from the past

Continual changes and advances have been made
Improvements that bring upgrades
But have you ever thought about the fact
That the camera has made a tremendous impact

What about books and magazines only in printed words
No pictures, just print, sounds a bit absurd
We take picture-taking ever so lightly
But its invention makes photos beam brightly

When we look at pictures taken from the past
We're reminded of how time goes by so fast
To our face they bring a smile
Of people we haven't seen in a while

Births, weddings, parties, and birthdays
Concerts, programs, sport events and school days
Sight-seeing, tours and especially vacations
All holidays and special celebrations

Good times and in company of family and friends
Taking pictures, there's just no end
Scenery, weather events, documents, and receipts
With the push of a button, we have pictures to keep

Now we have cameras in our phones
We can even make selfies, all alone
Galleries, yearbooks, and albums we store
As pictures and memories become more and more

So, the next time you pose and say "cheese"
Be thankful pictures can be taken with such ease

THE CLOCK

The clock was invented to tell time
Without it, time could not be defined
The clock is a useful gauging tool
Many learn to tell time in elementary school

Twelve numbers are strategically placed
And make what is called the clock's face
Whether on a wrist, table, or wall
It is purposed for the time to recall

We rely on clocks as a daily guide
For the exact time they provide
Imagine, however, how it would be
If there were no timepieces people could see

I fear confusion would definitely reign
A normal day would not be the same
Without time you would not know
When it's time to stay or time to go

Even if you knew when to begin
How would you know the time to end
How would you know if you were late
For an especially important date

How would you know when it's time for bed
You might rely on your body clock instead
If there is no alarm to beep
How would you awaken from time-set sleep

Parking meters, day planners and appointments to make
There'd be no need, we'd have to forsake
So, whenever you need to know the time
Be glad that clocks make it easy to find

THE LAWN MOWER

There is one invention many can appreciate
For time-saving service that it can generate

I am referring to the mower made to cut the grass
Whether pushing or riding, it cuts quite fast

Imagine, however, if there were no mower
Trying to cut grass would be an unmanageable chore

Grass would be unsightly and so very tall
Lawns would be unkempt; it would look terrible for all

But gladly we do have them to cut and trim the yards
Beautifying the landscape is not at all hard

THE PIANO

Of all the instruments, I must truly confess
The piano is the one with which I'm most impressed

Concert, baby grand, spinet, or console
Eighty-eight black and white keys make the keyboard

None of the keys can ever stand alone
It's the combination that makes the tones

Notes and tones create a harmonic array
Made by an artist who has been trained to play

Even more impressive is its versatility and range
The sounds from the piano are amazingly interchanged

Singers, musicians, and dancers use its accompaniment
Performances are enhanced as the piano compliments

The piano alone produces sweet melodic sounds
The piano alone awes and spellbounds

THE SEWING MACHINE

The sewing machine was invented to save time
For whatever needs one had in mind

With purchased fabric and coordinated thread
A pattern to use, you forge ahead

A single stitch becomes a seam
Separate pieces come together in a theme

Try on, make adjustments and repin
So that the fit will be exact in the end

Before you know it, stitch after stitch
What has developed is a completed outfit

A stitch in time really does define
The machine created your handmade design

A MIXED BAG

Opportunities, pleasures, and adaptations make life interesting. As one matures, the memories are more precious, the experiences are more appreciated, and the life changes are better understood. It is the variations of life that make it all worthwhile.

BE KIND

Kindness is universal, all can understand
We can use it at our command
Using manners and good graces
Put smiles on people's faces

Be kind and courteous and polite
Do it simply because it is right
Manners go far, yet cost nothing
For the recipient, though, it means something

People remember when you have been kind
Your act or deed never leaves their mind
And even if they don't know your name
They appreciate you just the same

When given the opportunity or chance
You see a need at a glance
Offer a seat or open the door
You will get smiles and thanks even more

It's so nice to be nice
Make it a habit
Don't think twice

BITES AND STINGS

Every day holds for us
The potential of bites and stings
They catch us unawares
With unexpectancies that they bring

It is vital, though, how you react
To the shock and pain
With immediate and correct attention
Healing you will gain

But discounting its importance
You choose to ignore
The problem soon will magnify
And the longer you will be sore

Prepare for the unexpected
The bites and the stings
Confront them quickly
A full resolution it will bring

COOKIES

Cookies are truly a delicacy
A miniature cake brings so much glee
These tasty cakes can be made at home
Or brought in the store in package form

The first cookie made was thought to be a test
To decide which oven temp would be best
There are six basic types
Sure to whet your appetites

Most are made of basic sugar dough
That can be made in other types, though
With ingredients combined in a bowl
They are cut, dropped, pressed, or rolled

These little treats are eaten by hand
Perhaps the reason for their great demand
Sugar, peanut butter, oatmeal, or chocolate chip
Are delicious with cold milk to sip

Cookies are what kids like to make
And can hardly wait to decorate
Families come together for cookie baking
This special time is memory making

What would Easter, Christmas and Valentine's Day be
Without hot out-of-the-oven treats, a guarantee
And don't forget Girl Scouts cookie time
You place your order and get them in time

Cookies bring a smile to everyone's face
They rank rather high in the dessert place

DAYLIGHT SAVING TIME

Daylight Saving Time is time manipulation
What it does create is discombobulation

With 24 hours in a day, what time does it save
All it does is confuses and alter ways

When we spring ahead to lose an hour
People become grumpy and sour

When we fall back, an hour we gain
Because it gets dark early, less daylight remains

So, what is the purpose of DST
Maybe Congress knows, don't ask me

DEFEAT, ADVERSITY AND PAIN

Defeat, adversity and pain
Can all wear you down
You try to overcome
You're knocked back to the ground

You easily become discouraged
But never ever give up
No matter the number of tries
No matter how hard or tough

Just keep on trying, never give in
Try and try and try again
For it is in the trying
You get a second wind

Wind enough to boost you
Wind enough to prevail
Wind enough to carry you
Determined not to fail

Disappointed in the results
That was your hardest test
Be encouraged still, you did not give up
You gave your absolute best

DREAMS

Your body is at rest
But your mind is certainly not
You can be in your own dreams
But sometimes you are not

Dreams are about people and places
Ordinary or special occasions

Dreams can recall the past
Be about the present
Or even foretell the future

Dreams can be scary or funny
Or make no sense at all

When you awaken
You remember the dream
You recall the details and specifics
As you replay them

Oddly enough, however
As quickly as you remember
You then soon forget

EXCEL

Autograph your work with excellence
For you may never know
The far-reaching benefits
That your labor will show

Let your work speak for itself
A self-portrait of you
Each time you work
Excel until you are through

You will never regret
In fact, the opposite is true
When you autograph your work with excellence
Your true character comes into view

FATIGUE

Fatigue is an enemy easy to recognize
It brings about changes anyone can surmise

You cannot fool the body; it has a mind of its own
Short nights, stress, wear and tear become easily known

It shows up in your mood, you are quick to irritate
Grumpy and short-tempered when rest you negate

Your body is lethargic, slower to respond
Without energy and more zombie-like you have become

Work hard, do not overdo, for balance is the key
De-stress with rest and pleasure, bring the body into harmony

Fatigue is an enemy, put it in its place
Use corrective action, fatigue will be displaced

GROOMED FOR SUCCESS

Appraise the actions and decisions
Evaluate the day
Decide which ones to discard
And which ones should stay

Hold yourself accountable
As you pursue your goals
Set a framework for success
The future you can mold

Decisions enhance your values
Becoming who you are
Values then become character
That will take you far

No matter what happens
Or what the future holds
Your good deeds and judgment
Put you in control

Change the things you can
Positively accept the rest
Success will pursue you
When you are your personal best

HUMILITY

An attitude of humility
Is what we should maintain
Rather than one
That is arrogant and vain

No one likes a person
Who boasts and is conceited
He thinks too highly of self
He thinks he is much needed

It is pride and vanity
That go before the fall
It is a matter of humility
That causes one to stand tall

If you truly want respect
If that is what you seek
Have a proper view of self
Be humble and meek

I AM SORRY

Sticks and stones may break your bones
But words can pierce the soul, changing the whole tone

When you say something and then you realize
That you have caused hurt, be quick to apologize

"I am sorry" are three little words
That openly express things you wish were not heard

Words can hurt if spoken without thought
Or if they were received in the way they should not

Those three words are magic; they change dispositions
And by your admission, they improve personal relations

Apologizing does more; it shows your concern
And from your experience, more about self you learn

If true character you show
You become a better person
From it you will grow

INFIDELITY

When you find out
That your mate has been untrue
Your world seems to crumble
Right in front of you

Your heart is broken
You hurt, you cry
You seek answers
You want to know why

You remember your vows
And the promises that were made
You have come together in union
With the groundwork you have laid

The proof is positive
The evidence is revealed
It is hard to express
The betrayal you feel

So, where you go from here
Depends on you two
To salvage and to save
To see your marriage through

It takes some time to mend
And to rebuild the trust
One heart to forgive
The other to do what it must

Move on with your marriage
With your spouse try to renew
Be honest and trustworthy
To your mate be true

KEEP YOUR WORD

If you make a promise
Always follow through
Stand on your word
And peace will follow you

It is important to the one
Your promise was made to
You will earn their respect
And they will trust you, too

A promise made and a promise kept
Does more than it seems
It is vital to others
And boosts your self-esteem

MAN UP

Man Up was on a T-shirt
I noticed just today
One thing came to mind
About thinking a different way

Man Up is admitting truth
Even if it is not good
Own up to your actions
Within, you know you should

There is something rather strange
About honesty and confession
It happens every time
It releases guilt and teaches a lesson

Press on until the next time
Think before you act
Man Up the first time
And you will be done with that

ME TIME

One might not have the luxury
Of a man-cave or she-shack
But we all must take time
To relax and kick back

Be it twenty minutes in the rocking chair
Or sixty minutes in the spa
Or a good soak in the bathtub
This "me time" will take you far

Take time for yourself
Mind, body, and soul
And then get back in the race
To be better in control

Relinquish the worries and cares
For a bit in your life
Be ye son, daughter
Sister, brother, or wife

You will be surprised
How this down time will reduce the stress
It will lift you up in no time
And peace of mind you will possess

MONEY

Money isn't everything
Yet, it indeed, helps a lot
To buy food, clothes, home and cars
And other stuff you got

Money takes care of necessities
And all that life requires
And many other things
That one also desires

But as the saying goes
Happiness is one thing
No matter how you try
That money itself cannot bring

It is giving to others
From the wealth you obtain
That your life is enriched
And satisfaction is gained

It is in giving and sharing
With those who do not have much
That you make a difference
With the hearts you touch

It's hard to believe
The sense of contentment
When for others, not self
That your money is spent

Give freely and give often
If you want to grow
Into the kind of person
Where meaning and purpose you will know

OPPOSITES

Opposites are words that are as different as can be
Words like
Start or stop
Bottom or top
Front or back
Plenty or lack
Wet or dry
Land or sky
Hot or cold
Young or old
Day or night
Wrong or right
Turmoil or rest
East or west
Naughty or nice
Cheap or for a price
Short or long
Weak or strong
Triumphant or tragic
Reality or magic
Sick or well
Heaven or hell
Black or white

Dull or bright
First or last
Slow or fast
Opposites are words that just cannot agree

PERSEVERE

Detours, false starts, and failures
Can surely defeat
Yet failures in one's life
Have something to teach

Life can be put on hold
When you stay down and get by
rather than choose to resist
press on and retry

Do not grow weary
keep toiling and persevere
what you work toward
will soon be near

Do not lose heart despite setbacks
remember your purpose and work your plan
more times than not
your accomplishment is at hand

PRIDE, DETERMINATION AND RESILIENCE

Pride, determination, and resilience are three important traits
That can prove helpful, allow me to demonstrate

Pride is a sense of worth, but not the puffed-up kind
It is a sense of accomplishment for the task you did find

Determination is stick-to-itiveness no matter the test
It is deciding not to quit, it is giving your absolute best

Resilience is bouncing back when things don't go as planned
It is not giving up despite the outcome
and dealing with what is at hand

Pride, determination, and resilience
Strive to have all three
For they build the type of character
To live successfully

SEND?

There is a "send" button on your device,
And no matter where you are,
The message is sent
Quite rapidly and quite far.

Unless you are sure,
Do not push send,
Once it had been sent,
You cannot rescind.

Read the written message carefully,
Make sure it is exact,
Consider the recipient
And how they might react.

Once you push the button,
It is in cyberland,
There's nothing you can do,
It is out of your hands.

I'm speaking from experience,
For it has happened to me.
Think, text, rethink and push "send",
You'll have no regrets, you'll be worry-free.

SPRING CLEANING

Spring cleaning conjures up the promise
Of a fresh start
It's light, refreshing and uplifting
It's what sets this season apart

It's time to open the windows
To let the fresh air in
It's time to lose the heavy
Winter stuff that's been

It's time to clear the closet
Remove unwanted clothes
It's time to put out new plants
Changing the landscape that grows

Spring is time
To renew and spruce up the home
To restore its beauty in a revised form
To release unwanted items, clothes, and things
To receive vitality that only Spring can bring

THERMOSTAT OR THERMOMETER

A thermostat controls the temperature
And the temperature controls the thermometer
They can be likened to people we know
Those in control and those who go with the flow

The thermometer person is not in control
He doesn't prepare so he has no goals
When things don't go as he wants them to
There's no Plan B and he doesn't know what to do

Situations dictate how he will act
To sit back idly or instantly react
If things get hot, he panics and sweats
He's full of doubt, worry and regret

The thermostat person is in control
Of his life's responsibilities and goals
He knows his life is in his hands
By planning to prepare and preparing to plan

Prayerfully and positively, he proceeds
He diligently works toward meeting his needs
He is persistent and patient and he doesn't give up
Even though times may be a little tough

He works hard and knows when to stop
He relies on God to do what he cannot

TO TEACH

To teach
Is to first recognize the awesome responsibility
To educate and impact
Students that have been entrusted to you

To teach

Is to impart knowledge
By building on a foundation
For students to gain academically

To teach
Is to instill a love of learning
And understanding how doors can open
To possibilities and opportunities

To teach
Is to encourage a belief in one's own capabilities
And what can be accomplished
From one's own inspiration

To teach
Is to model the traits for others to see
The characteristics needed
To in life succeed

Once students learn the skills, want to learn
Believe in themselves, and develop good character
Anything they desire is within reach

WHAT TO DO

What if you don't know what to do
When many conflicting thoughts come into view
No assurance or help is on cue
And advising friends are too few
Because a decision is soon due
You've worked yourself into a stew
You so much wish you had a clue
Your molehill became a mountain – it just grew
You must weigh your options, decide which to pursue
Do what you think is truly best for you
Talk it through, break through, follow through
And soon you will know what to do

WHAT'S ON THE INSIDE

Do not look upon the vessel
But what it holds
Gives us great insight
As a Hebrew proverb has told

As humans we are guilty
At looking at the cover
When it's what on the inside
We must discover

In looking on the outside
We begin to cast our doubts
Our thinking could be clouded
On what character is about

Because someone looks different
From what we think they should
We become judgmental
And that person is misunderstood

Until we get to know them
Put misconceptions aside
Dismiss the outer appearance
Seek to know what's inside

MY JOURNEY

My journey is a culmination of my life experiences – family, upbringing, education, and career. As a mother and grandmother, I can so appreciate my parents and my grandmother, instrumental role models, who taught much that has impacted my life. They left indelible marks on my mind and heart. I have learned much, inside and outside of the classroom. My life has not always been smooth sailing, but the challenges have strengthened me and deepened my faith. God has truly blessed my life.

DINNER WITH THE FORMER PRESIDENT

If with former President Obama I could dine
I'd consider it an honor to share his time
I 'd be so excited, there'd be little eating
I would be so enthralled in our meeting

I'd ask many questions of him
I know he would respond to each of them

I would like to know his biggest obstacle
His most difficult decision
His greatest pleasure
His biggest disappointment
What he would have changed if he could
What is the one thing he would hope America knows about him
How he would want to be remembered

After all the interrogation, I would lay it on the line
An African American president, I never imagined in my lifetime

I would tell him that he not only served one term
Dutifully he completed two
How I admired his intelligence, his character and courage
That I know how hard he tried
To unify the parties to work for the people
How he held his office
With dignity, respect, and fortitude

How he truly made a difference
And has made a lasting impact on our nation
That he will be long remembered
For who he is and for what he has done
How I wish him well
He, his beautiful daughters, and his wife Michelle

FINE CHINA

The cabinet and the buffet in the dining room
Contain my fine china that could become an heirloom

They have their own purpose and storage place
Not used often, they would be hard to replace

The purchase of this china, originally was a must
But what it does primarily is collect its share of dust

Because it is so delicate, I use it once a year
For special occasions only, these dishes are so dear

When used, they are hand washed, stored and concealed
Until the same time next year when their beauty is revealed

MA-MA

My grandmother was extra special, so precious and dear
She lived life to the fullest, all ninety-nine years

From her so much I learned, not just by what she said
But on a day-to-day basis, the type of life she led

She was wise beyond her years as it appeared to me
Her godly advice helped me a different perspective to see

Her formal education ended at eighth grade
But one would never know that by the attainments she made

When I was young, she advised me to tithe and save
Never knowing when they will come, prepare for rainy days

She never had a credit card way back then
She believed you pay in full, or simply do not spend

Ma-Ma traveled around the world, places she had never seen
She would always share her experiences,
presenting on a slide show screen

Each year my siblings and I, to Kansas City we would go
There, only for a short time, how we all did grow

She made summers so much fun, time went by too fast
Picnics, outdoor theater, neighborhood friends,
made for times we wanted to last

Ma-Ma was a classy lady who cared about her dress
Polished nails, Sunday hats, and furs, nevertheless

Her hair was so well kept, she was a pretty blond
She colored it herself, had never been to a salon

Ma-Ma had a sense of humor, she would tell the same old jokes
She would laugh so hard, we thought she just might choke

She could cook anything and make it taste great
Especially her burnt sugar gravy, apple
and lemon pies and pound cake

My grandmother did the absolute best
with the little that she had
She was generous and kind to others,
being around her made me glad

Ma-Ma was awe-inspiring, a legacy she did make
Why wouldn't I look up to her, after all, I am her namesake

MESSY KITCHEN

I have collected recipes for a long time
My obsession started around 1969
I have recipes and cookbooks galore
There is no space for even one more

When through magazines pages I flip
An enticing-looking recipe I snip
I always wonder as I look
If my dish will look like the one in the book

With recipe in hand, I give it a try
Listing ingredients that I need to buy
I assemble what I will use
Bowls, mixer and my measuring tools

Step by step I follow directions
Hoping the result will be perfection
I carefully, stir, mix and measure
Experimenting brings me pleasure

It is when I'm finished, and I look around
It appears a tornado has touched down
How could I have made such a mess
I sure hope this dish passes the test

I commence to clean and straighten up
Down to the last measuring cup
Is this a recipe that I will repeat
My family decides if I discard or keep

MY FRIEND

To have a friend is to be one
You can know a true friend by what she has done

She is someone in whom you can rely
Your needs she will not deny

She goes the distance and the miles
Because your friendship is so worthwhile

She knows when to sit and listen
And give her undivided attention

She is someone you can trust
Honesty and sincerity are her musts

With her there is much to share
You know she truly does care

She is so close she knows you well
If something is wrong, she can tell

She knows your faults that are real
Despite them, she loves you still

I thank God for my faithful friend
Through it all, she's there to the end

I hope she feels the same about me
A loyal friend, undeniably

MY INTERESTS

Writing poems and personal cards
Are expressions from my heart
Once I am inspired the writing begins
And before I know it, I have come to the end

Solving ciphers, jumbles and word finds
And crossword puzzles of all kinds
Sudoku with numbers to nine
All seem to sharpen my mind

Reading books is a time to relax
Yet I still learn so many facts
A cup of coffee and a book to caress
Always calms any level of stress

There is something about written print
That expresses an author's accomplishment
Technology and computers may be the trend
However, all I need for inspiration is paper and pen

MY PET, MY VET

To pay for college tuition
Taking time off to work was his intention

In a matter of weeks, Uncle Sam had a plan
To draft this eligible 22-year-old man

He soon sent special greetings to him
Acknowledging the upcoming meeting between them

The news came as a shock to his mother
Yet, veterans were his two older brothers

So off to basic camp he went
Where eight whole weeks would be spent

From there he went to Fort Sam Houston
For medic training at the base institution

Two years spent in Alaska at Fort Richardson
Time went swiftly, until his service was done

Mountain glacier training in the frigid cold
Snow skiing and riverboat driving, doing as told

He was promoted to Sergeant E-5
With a sense of commitment and drive

He looks back on the three years served
Being honorably discharged as he deserved

He served his country with dignity and duty
My husband, US Army veteran, he is truly

OUR FAMILY

Family is significant in extending the family tree
Ours is a small one, hubby, three kids and me

Our oldest is a son, so special and loved
He was the first child we spoiled for a while
He is out-going, pleasant, athletic and smart
He enjoys golfing, UT football, and Kappas with all his heart

Our middle is another son, so special and loved
Much like my dad he never met
Traits and skills from him he did get
He has a love of music, to his heart he has been true
He studied and prepared for doing what he loves to do

Our third child is a daughter, so special and loved
As our only girl, she brought joy to our world
She has beauty, inside and out
And a heart of gold, no doubt

All three are gifts from God and are as different as can be
Wouldn't want it any other way, we're grateful for our three

QVC

I love to shop on QVC
They offer so much just for me
They show products that demonstrate
How using them will make life great
So much to choose from, some I want
Others not as enticing, so I don't
I let the remote control me
I like the many things I see
I tell myself it is what I need
This idea in my head I believe
Once I decide, I make my selection
Then I follow the 1-800 directions
When he brings boxes through the door
He realizes I have been shopping more
He is putting QVC on spousal control
For to me too much they have sold
I am going to have to
Quit
Viewing
Channels that allure

RECIPES

I have collected recipes
Since my young adult life
When I see a recipe
I snip, snip, snip without thinking twice

In my senior years
What I now realize
I'm really a big-time hoarder
Just one that is organized

I have collected recipes
Since the nineteen sixties
Stored away in boxes
I could never use all these

In addition to loose recipes
I have cookbooks galore
What's so terrible about it
I'm still collecting more

In boxes, in cabinets, on bookshelves
Under the bed, or wherever
I need to put a stop to this
But I know I'll never

REMEMBERING

I enjoy writing simple rhymes
To recall my most memorable times

I remember my baby sister as she came through the door
With my brothers and me, we became four

I remember fighting in fifth grade
Not knowing then a best friend I had made

I remember walking to school each day
Unless it rained, Daddy was on his way

I remember twirling and playing Pop the Whip
That broke my front tooth 'cause my playmate lost her grip

I remember hot summer train rides to Kansas City
To visit Ma-Ma who was a great cook, wise and witty

I remember winning the City Beautiful essay contest
Explaining how Memphis could enhance Beale Street best

I remember that being Drum Major was quite grand
My high-stepping marches led the entire band

I remember arts and crafts and the fun of making things
That developed into a love of using the sewing machine

I remember riding the bus to LeMoyne College
For there is where I gained my teaching knowledge

I remember meeting and dating my college friend
Not realizing with him my life I would spend

I remember my sisterhood of AKA
To her I will be loyal all the day

I remember getting married in cold December
Fifty-five years ago, but I still remember

I remember Alaska's beauty of mountains and snow
Army life and a friendship that continues to grow

I remember traveling across our nation
In the VW bug, our mode of transportation

I remember birthing our number one son
Into our lives he brought joy and fun

I remember unexpectantly losing my dad
My pregnant life for a while was so sad

I remember giving birth to son number two
He had a gift of music that tremendously grew

I remember the baby girl that we always wanted
The pigtails, ribbons, and lace that she flaunted

I remember being pushed down as we roller skated
With a broken right shoulder, I was incapacitated

I remember our family moving across the state
For the Oak Ridge job that he decided to take

I remember the big celebration of our 25th year
A joyous occasion of renewing our vows, so dear

I remember thirty-two years of teaching classes
Hoping I've made an impact on the masses

Life for me has been bitter-sweet
God has been good, and Satan I will defeat

I pray to God that the rest of my days
Will be pleasing to Him in all my ways

TEACHING

Teaching is something I did for many years
A passion from the beginning, it appears

I "taught" my siblings as they sat on the stairs
Answering my questions, without any cares

Education was my major for the career I would pursue
As the learning and anticipation grew

I taught different grade levels and subjects, too
Long nights of planning and grading I committed to do

Students were challenged to always do their best
Most worked hard and settled for nothing less

Teaching, to me, was the most important job there was
Molding and motivating became my personal cause

I hope that time in my class was well spent
Preparing students for the future was my intent

Teaching was so rewarding for me
Seeing students learn and progress was the key

The greatest honor that I have received
Was the appreciation expressed by students and parents, indeed

THE GOLDEN YEARS

I met him in college, he was my sweetheart
We dated three years, and didn't want to be apart

On December 30, 1966, he and I said "I do"
To our marriage, we committed to be true

Our marriage is not perfect, but neither are we
It's about give and take and agreeing to disagree

He eats to live, I live to eat
He likes salty, I prefer sweet

I like HGTV or movies with happy endings
He likes sports and movies that suspend

I'm attentive to detail, he's hurry up and go
I like to spend, he wants to save; it works, though

I like his sense of humor; I like to hear "Yes, Dear"
He likes to make me laugh; his motives are sincere

Marriage is demonstrating love every day
Yet accepting the other's different ways

The greatest compliment that our son has given
Is to be like his dad to his children, so driven

The greatest compliment that I can send
If given a second chance, I would do it over again

God has been good, for blessings we have amassed
For 55 years as man and wife, each year better than the last

THE GROCERY STORE

Because we must eat each day
This store is the place I cannot stay away
Grocery stores are set up quite well
For all the groceries they want to sell

I make selections as my cart is filled
As there is enough to prepare my meals
If I have planned before I go
The list and coupons help me so

The cost of the food is so extremely high
I can't stay on budget as much as I try
Although I tend to complain
I know next time will be the same

Then there's the guilt that I've done wrong
Having to toss food that I have kept too long
I begin to adjust my misguided attitude
And fill it instead with one of gratitude

"TO DO" LIST

I begin the workday by making a list
So what needs to get done, I don' t miss
With good intentions I really do try
But before long time has passed by

The list has dwindled to only a few
I still have so much to do
I know one thing that might help
Is to finish one job before I go to the next

I then start to make excuses
For poor time management uses
Putting things off for another date
Delaying still as I procrastinate

When I think I'll do it tomorrow
I'm just looking for time to borrow
It would be helpful if I'd organize
And decide which chores to prioritize

I know my shortcomings, I have a few
Until I get better, unfinished chores I will pursue

WHERE DID IT GO?

I had it first in my right hand
So I could pick up the hot pan
Possibly shifting things around
I left the room for just a sec
For something else I had to check
I came back through the door
And it was not where it was before
I kept looking in the same place
Perhaps I put it elsewhere in haste
In turning things upside down
That potholder is nowhere to be found
Over, under, around and through
My search continues as I pursue
I check the cabinet and the floor
I even open the refrigerator door
Then I wonder if I'm losing my mind
That potholder is so hard to find
But I calm down and say a prayer
Before I know it, there it is, right there
I just don't understand
That potholder was in my left hand

ACKNOWLEDGEMENTS

I would like to acknowledge and thank those who played a role in my second publication.

Several friends and family encouraged me to publish.

Dear friends Arlene Banfield and La Royce Beatty gave of their time again to edit and offer suggestions.

Lisa Berry and my grandson have been a tremendous help with technology.

And I would like to thank my husband for his patience and support.

ABOUT THE AUTHOR

Avar Hurd James was born in Memphis, Tennessee.

She earned her B.A. from LeMoyne Owen College, M.A. from the University of Memphis, and Ed.S. from Lincoln Memorial University. She has taught in Memphis City Schools and is retired from Alcoa City Schools. She also served as an Educational Consultant with the Tennessee Department of Education.

Avar and her husband reside in Maryville, Tennessee. They are the parents of three children and four grandchildren.

This is her second publication.